Level 1 | Part 2

# STUDENT ACTIVITIES MANUAL
# 作業簿
## for

# Chinese Link

# 中 文 天 地
Zhōng　　Wén　　Tiān　　Dì

*Beginning Chinese*

Second Edition

Traditional Character Version

吳素美　　于月明　　張燕輝　　田維忠
Sue-mei Wu　　Yueming Yu　　Yanhui Zhang　　Weizhong Tian

**Prentice Hall**

Boston　Columbus　Indianapolis　New York　San Francisco　Upper Saddle River
Amsterdam　Cape Town　Dubai　London　Madrid　Milan　Munich　Paris　Montréal　Toronto
Delhi　Mexico City　São Paulo　Sydney　Hong Kong　Seoul　Singapore　Taipei　Tokyo

*Senior Acquisitions Editor:* Rachel McCoy
*Editorial Assistant:* Noha Amer
*Publishing Coordinator:* Kathryn Corasaniti
*Executive Marketing Manager:* Kris Ellis-Levy
*Senior Marketing Manager:* Denise Miller
*Marketing Coordinator:* William J. Bliss
*Senior Media Editor:* Samantha Alducin
*Development Editor:* Christina Shafermeyer
*Development Editor for Assessment:* Melissa Marolla Brown
*Media Editor:* Meriel Martinez
*Senior Managing Editor:* Mary Rottino
*Associate Managing Editor:* Janice Stangel
*Senior Production Project Manager:* Manuel Echevarria
*Senior Manufacturing and Operations Manager, Arts and Sciences:* Nick Sklitsis
*Operations Specialist:* Cathleen Petersen
*Senior Art Director:* Pat Smythe
*Art Director:* Miguel Ortiz
*Cover Image:* Jochen Helle
*Full-Service Project Management:* Margaret Chan, Graphicraft Limited
*Printer/Binder:* Bind-Rite Graphics
*Cover Printer:* Lehigh-Phoenix Color/Hagerstown
*Publisher:* Phil Miller

Copyright © 2011 Pearson Education, Inc., publishing as Prentice Hall, 1 Lake St., Upper Saddle River, NJ 07458. All rights reserved. Manufactured in the United States of America. This publication is protected by Copyright, and permission should be obtained from the publisher prior to any prohibited reproduction, storage in a retrieval system, or transmission in any form or by any means, electronic, mechanical, photocopying, recording, or likewise. To obtain permission(s) to use material from this work, please submit a written request to Pearson Education, Inc., Permissions Department, 1 Lake St., Upper Saddle River, NJ 07458.

This book was set in 12/15 Sabon by Graphicraft Ltd., Hong Kong.

Printed in the United States of America

**Prentice Hall**
is an imprint of

**PEARSON**

www.pearsonhighered.com

ISBN 10: 0-205-74138-X
ISBN 13: 978-0-205-74138-0

## 目錄　CONTENTS

**Preface** v

**Lesson 12**　Making Requests　　　　第十二課　請求　　　　1

**Lesson 13**　Clothes and Shopping　　第十三課　衣服、逛街　　7

**Lesson 14**　Birthdays and Celebrations　第十四課　生日和慶祝　13

**Lesson 15**　Location and Position　　第十五課　地點和位置　　19

**Lesson 16**　Hobbies and Sports　　　第十六課　愛好和運動　　25

**Lesson 17**　Weather and Seasons　　第十七課　天氣和四季　　31

**Lesson 18**　Travel and Transportation　第十八課　旅行和交通　　37

**Lesson 19**　Health and Medicine　　　第十九課　健康和醫藥　　43

**Lesson 20**　Renting an Apartment　　第二十課　看房和租房　　49

**Lesson 21**　Future Plans　　　　　　第二十一課　未來計畫　　55

**Lesson 22**　Arts and Culture　　　　第二十二課　藝術和文化　61

# 前言 PREFACE

The second edition of the *Student Activities Manual* for the *Chinese Link* contains homework assignments for each lesson in the main textbook. Homework activities are divided among listening exercises, character exercises, grammar exercises, and comprehensive exercises.

Thanks to the many instructors and students who provided valuable feedback on the first edition, the second edition incorporates several new features that we believe will make the materials more effective and easier to use. These new features are highlighted below:

1. For more efficiency and convenience, the **Workbook** is now divided into two separate volumes, the *Student Activities Manual* and *Character Book*.

    The new edition of the *Student Activities Manual* now provides a greater variety of exercises to consolidate what students have learned for each lesson. It incorporates listening, character, grammar and comprehensive exercises into each lesson's homework.

    The *Character Book* now combines both the traditional and simplified character versions.

2. More **challenging and authentic materials** have been added to the listening exercises. Situational dialogues have been created for each lesson that incorporate its themes, expressions, and its pragmatic settings of the lesson. Dialogues also contain some vocabulary and expressions that the students have not yet studied in the hope that these situational dialogues can challenge them from the very beginning and help them develop the skill of picking out useful information even if they don't fully understand everything they hear. This helps develop an important survival skill for students who will encounter real-life settings in Chinese society through study abroad, travel, or interaction with Chinese communities in their own countries.

3. At the end of each lesson's exercises, a **Progress Checklist** is included so that instructors and students can check that the students have accomplished the goals of the lesson and acquired the competencies that the lesson was designed to help them learn.

Sue-mei Wu 吳素美, Ph.D.
Lead author of *Chinese Link*
Carnegie Mellon University

# Lesson 12    Making Requests
# 第十二課 請求

## I. Listening Exercises

**12-1**   Listen and choose the correct meaning for each sentence you hear.

1. a. He wants to know whether I want to have dinner at his home.
   b. He wants to know if he can have dinner at my home.
   c. He told me that I should have dinner at his home.

2. a. You should drink more coffee.
   b. You should not drink coffee.
   c. You should drink less coffee.

3. a. Xiao Li wants me to drive him to the library to borrow two English literature books.
   b. Xiao Li doesn't want to drive to the school's library to borrow two English literature books.
   c. Xiao Li wants to drive to the school's library to borrow two English literature books.

4. a. It will take five days to drive from New York[1] to Los Angeles.[2]
   b. It won't take five days to drive from New York to Los Angeles.
   c. We shouldn't drive from New York to Los Angeles.

5. a. I will go home to see my mother in May next year.
   b. I will go home to see my mother in May this year.
   c. I will go home to see my mother in June this year.

6. a. Tomorrow I can use the computer[3] my friend lent me to write an email to Xiao Wang.
   b. Tomorrow I will use the computer Xiao Wang lent me to write an email to my friend.
   c. Tomorrow I cannot use the computer my friend lent me to write an email to Xiao Wang.

*Notes:*  1. 紐約 [Niǔyuē]: New York
   2. 洛杉磯 [Luòshānjī]: Los Angeles
   3. 電腦 [diànnǎo]: computer

**12-2** Listen to the dialogue between 方明英 and 丁文. Then choose whether the following statements are true or false.

1. 丁文很想看這個中國電影*。     True     False
2. 丁文明天下午沒有課。     True     False
3. 每天下午有車從宿舍到中美圖書館。     True     False
4. 丁文要跟方明英一起看電影。     True     False

*Note:* 電影 [diànyǐng]: movie

**12-3** Listen to the challenge dialogue. Though there may be some words and phrases that are unfamiliar to you, see if you can understand the general meaning by using what you have learned. Then choose whether the following statements are true or false.

1. 本樂's roommate is coming back from China.     True     False
2. 于影 is going to give a presentation tomorrow morning.     True     False
3. 本樂 will let 于影 borrow his notebook computer.     True     False

**12-4** Listen to the challenge dialogue again and choose the best answer for each of the following questions.

1. What is 本樂 doing now?
   a. He is surfing the Internet.
   b. He is having dinner.
   c. He is going to the airport.
   d. He is reading a book.

2. Who is back from Beijing?
   a. 于影     b. 本樂     c. 本樂's girlfriend     d. 本樂's roommate

3. When will 本樂 and 于影 meet again?
   a. Tonight at 8:00.
   b. Tomorrow morning.
   c. This afternoon at 5:00.
   d. Tomorrow afternoon at 5:00.

Name: _____ Date: _____

## II. Character Exercises

**12-5** Choose the correct simplified form for each of the following characters.

1. 飛   a. 乐   b. 从   c. 飞
2. 習   a. 书   b. 习   c. 时
3. 開   a. 几   b. 儿   c. 开
4. 應   a. 应   b. 会   c. 么
5. 練   a. 给   b. 练   c. 绍
6. 進   a. 还   b. 这   c. 进

**12-6** Write the Chinese characters for the following phrases.

1. wǒ děi qù jīchǎng jiē wǒ mèimei   _____
2. yīnggāi méi wèntí   _____
3. wǒde Zhōngwén jìnbù le   _____
4. wǒde chē shì báisè de   _____
5. tíng zài wǔ hào tíngchē chǎng   _____

## III. Grammar Exercises

**12-7** Choose an optative verb from the box to complete the following sentences. Note that more than one answer may be possible in some cases.

> 要，想，應該，得，能，可以，會

1. 他們 _____ 坐飛機從紐約來這兒玩兒。
2. 我的爸爸媽媽都 _____ 說中文，你 _____ 跟他們說中文。
3. 她 _____ 會開手排擋的車。
4. 我今天晚上 _____ 借你的車嗎?

Lesson 12 ■ *Making Requests*   3

**12-8** Use negative optative verbs to turn the following positive sentences into negative sentences.

1. 我要在早上六點起床。
   _____

2. 我們想多喝點茶。
   _____

3. 小美應該多練習開車。
   _____

4. 我能借老師的書。
   _____

5. 在宿舍可以看電視。
   _____

6. 老師今天會晚點兒下課。
   _____

7. 你得開車去機場。
   _____

8. 她應該少喝咖啡，多喝水。
   _____

## IV. Comprehensive Exercises

**12-9** Read the following passage and then answer the questions below.

我叫李紅英，我在華中大學學工程。我的爸爸媽媽都是中國人，可是我在美國出生[1]，也在美國長大[2]。我小的時候，爸爸媽媽說我應該學中文。可是我不喜歡學中文。爸爸媽媽跟我說中文的時候，我總是[3]跟他們說英文。

上大學以後我認識到[4]學中文很重要，於是[5]我非常想學中文了。去年八月的時候，我去問華中大學中文系的王老師我應該上哪個中文班。王老師問我的中文怎麼樣。我說我能說一點兒中文，可是我一個中文字也不會寫。王老師說我應該在一年級[6]學中文。

*Notes:*
1. 出生 [chūshēng]: born
2. 長大 [zhǎngdà]: grow up
3. 總是 [zǒngshì]: always
4. 認識到 [rènshidào]: realize
5. 於是 [yúshì]: therefore
6. 一年級 [yī niánjí]: 1st year

1. 李紅英在哪個大學學習？她學什麼？

_____

2. 李紅英小的時候跟爸爸媽媽說中文嗎？

_____

3. 上中文課以前，李紅英會說中文、寫中文嗎？

_____

4. 王老師說李紅英應該上哪個中文班？

_____

Lesson 12 ■ *Making Requests*

**12-10** Answer the following questions in Chinese.

1. 你想不想學二年級的中文?

2. 你會不會說法文？日文呢?

3. 你會不會開手排擋的車?

4. 你可以不可以晚上十一點以後去圖書館借書?

## Progress Checklist

After this lesson, you should be able to use Chinese to:

( ) borrow something from someone,

( ) tell others what they should or should not do,

( ) ask others what they would like to do,

( ) ask/give permission to do something,

( ) ask/tell about someone's capabilities for doing something (e.g., driving a car, language skills),

( ) express the possibility of something occurring.

Name: _____ Date: _____

# Lesson 13  Clothes and Shopping
# 第十三課 衣服、逛街

## I. Listening Exercises

**13-1** Listen to the dialogue between 方明飛 and 店員. Then choose whether the following statements are true or false.

1. 方明飛想買一件襯衫。　　　　　　True　　False

2. 店員給他看看藍色和黑色的褲子。　True　　False

3. 方明飛喜歡黑色的褲子。　　　　　True　　False

4. 店員說黃襯衫很好看。　　　　　　True　　False

5. 方明飛說黑色的襯衫很不錯。　　　True　　False

**13-2** Listen to the sentences and fill in the blanks with the words you hear.

1. 我想買一____ 襯衫 _____ 一條褲子。

2. 你 _____ 看看。我 ____ 這件好嗎?

3. 這條裙子 _____?

4. 請 _____。

5. 我 _____ 喜歡黑色的大衣。

**13-3** Listen to the challenge dialogue. Though there may be some words and phrases that are unfamiliar to you, see if you can understand the general meaning by using what you have learned. Then choose whether the following statements are true or false.

1. They are talking about a computer.　　　　　　True　　　False

2. 愛紅's boyfriend doesn't buy skirts for her.　　　True　　　False

3. 愛紅 is wearing a green skirt.　　　　　　　　True　　　False

**13-4** Listen to the challenge dialogue again and choose the best answer for each of the following questions.

1. Where are 愛紅 and 子英 now?
    a. They are in a clothing store.
    b. They are in a restaurant.
    c. They are sitting in front of a computer.
    d. They are in the movie theater.

2. What color of skirt does 愛紅 like?
    a. Green.
    b. Red.
    c. White.
    d. Yellow.

3. What would 愛紅 like to do now?
    a. She is going to the store to buy another skirt.
    b. She is going to return the clothes she doesn't like.
    c. She is going to try on the skirt she bought.
    d. She is going to look at clothes online with 子英.

## II. Character Exercises

**13-5** Choose the correct simplified form for each of the following characters.

1. 襯   a. 衫   b. 衬   c. 见
2. 覺   a. 觉   b. 黄   c. 帮
3. 買   a. 卖   b. 买   c. 票
4. 褲   a. 衣   b. 裙   c. 裤
5. 讓   a. 让   b. 试   c. 说

**13-6** Match the Pinyin with the corresponding Chinese character.

_____ 1. wèi      a. 穿
_____ 2. chuān    b. 裙
_____ 3. tiáo     c. 试
_____ 4. mǎi      d. 位
_____ 5. qún      e. 條
_____ 6. ràng     f. 衫
_____ 7. shì      g. 買
_____ 8. shān     h. 讓

## III. Grammar Exercises

**13-7** Write the correct measure words.

1. 一 ____ 褲子
2. 兩 ____ 襯衫
3. 三 ____ 鞋
4. 四 ____ 裙子
5. 五 ____ 牛仔褲
6. 六 ____ 運動衫
7. 七 ____ 小狗
8. 八 ____ 電影票

**13-8** Answer the questions below using 或者.

1. 你回家以後想做什麼?

   _____

2. 這張電影票是誰的?

   _____

3. 我們去哪個餐館吃飯?

   _____

4. 你喜歡黃襯衫嗎?

   _____

Name: _____ Date: _____

## IV. Comprehensive Exercises

**13-9** Complete the following dialogues, using the clues given in parentheses.

1. **A:** 你說那件襯衫怎麼樣?

   **B:** _____。(Let me have a look.)

2. **A:** 我應該穿幾號的?

   **B:** _____。(Try a size 6 or a size 7.)

3. **A:** 我不知道這個電影是說什麼的。

   **B:** _____。(I'll give you a little introduction.)

4. **A:** 上海春捲真好吃。

   **B:** 真的嗎? _____。(I'll taste it as well.)

5. **A:** 手排擋的車我還不會開。

   **B:** _____。(You should learn how to drive.)

**13-10** Describe a recent shopping trip. (Use approximately 80–100 characters.)

_____

_____

_____

_____

_____

_____

_____

# Progress Checklist

After this lesson, you should be able to use Chinese to:

( ) name different types of clothing,

( ) express what you would like to buy,

( ) express what color(s) you like,

( ) provide your opinions of clothing (e.g., looks good/bad, expensive/cheap, etc.),

( ) ask/tell how much something costs.

# Lesson 14    Birthdays and Celebrations
# 第十四課 生日和慶祝

## I. Listening Exercises

**14-1**  Listen to the sentences and fill in the blanks with the words you hear.

1. 三月十八日是我的_____。

2. 我今年_____，_____二十歲。

3. _____是我的生日_____。請你_____。

**14-2**  Listen to the dialogue. Then choose the best answer for each of the following questions.

1. How old is Xingxing?
    a. She is twenty.
    b. She is twenty-one.
    c. She is twenty-two.
    d. She is twenty-three.

2. When is Mingming's birthday party?
    a. This Friday.     b. Next Friday.     c. This Saturday.     d. Next Saturday.

3. How old is Mingming going to be?
    a. Twenty.     b. Twenty-one.     c. Twenty-two.     d. Twenty-three.

4. Who does Mingming say will also be coming to his birthday party?
    a. Lots of his friends.
    b. His father and his girlfriend.
    c. His classmates and his brother.
    d. His sister and his sister's boyfriend.

5. Who will make the birthday cake?
    a. His roommate.     b. His friend.     c. Xingxing.     d. His mom.

**14-3** Listen to the challenge dialogue. Though there may be some words and phrases that are unfamiliar to you, see if you can understand the general meaning by using what you have learned. Then choose whether the following statements are true or false.

1. They are talking about last year's Chinese New Year party.   True   False

2. 愛紅 is going to 子英's party tonight.   True   False

3. 子英 is going to learn how to make a birthday cake and a Chinese New Year cake.   True   False

**14-4** Listen to the challenge dialogue again and choose the best answer for each of the following questions.

1. What does 愛紅 give 子英 as a birthday present?
    a. A new book.
    b. A birthday cake.
    c. Dumplings.
    d. A pack of tea.

2. How does 愛紅 know about 子英's birthday?
    a. She heard it from 子英's roommate.
    b. She is 子英's roommate.
    c. 子英 told her in the past.
    d. She heard it from 子英's boyfriend.

3. When is 愛紅's birthday?
    a. On the 10th of last month.
    b. On the 10th of next month.
    c. Today.
    d. During the Christmas holiday.

Name: _____ Date: _____

## II. Character Exercises

**14-5** Match each simplified character with its traditional form.

_____ 1. 岁    a. 會

_____ 2. 过    b. 為

_____ 3. 为    c. 圖

_____ 4. 参    d. 氣

_____ 5. 气    e. 參

_____ 6. 会    f. 歲

_____ 7. 图    g. 過

**14-6** Write the following Pinyin sentences in Chinese characters.

1. Wǒde shēngrì shì yīyuè sān shí hào, xīngqīsì.

   _____

2. Zhè shì nǐde péngyou sòng nǐde dà dàngāo ma?

   _____

3. Nǐ jīnnián duō dà? Wǒ jīnnián shíjiǔ suì.

   _____

Lesson 14 ■ *Birthdays and Celebrations*    15

## III. Grammar Exercises

**14-7** Fill in the blanks according to this year's calendar.

1. 今年春節 [Chūnjié] (Spring Festival / Chinese New Year) 是 _____ (date), _____ (day of the week) 。

2. 今天是 _____ (date), _____ (day of the week) 。

3. 下個星期日是 _____ (date) 。

4. 今年的感恩節 [Gǎn'ēnjié] (Thanksgiving) 是 _____ (date) _____ (day of the week) 。

5. 聖誕節 [Shèngdànjié] (Christmas) 是 _____ (date) _____ (day of the week) 。

6. 我的生日是 _____ (date), 今年在 _____ (day of the week) 。

**14-8** Rewrite the following sentences to include 為 and another person.

1. 我要做蛋糕。
   _____

2. 我媽媽想買襯衫。
   _____

3. 小明要去圖書館借中文書。
   _____

4. 妹妹要做炒麵。
   _____

5. 我們想開中文班的晚會。
   _____

## IV. Comprehensive Exercises

**14-9** Complete the following sentences, using the clues given in parentheses.

1. 下個星期日我要 _____ 。
   (hold a birthday party for my friend)

2. 你可以 _____ ?
   (make an order of Chinese dumplings for me)

3. 後天是媽媽的生日，我要 _____ 。
   (buy a very pretty shirt for her)

**14-10** You've called a friend to invite them to your roommate's birthday party next Saturday. Your friend wasn't home so you left a message. Write down what you said in your message. Try to include the following words and expressions (as well as other words and expressions you have learned).

生日　空　晚會　月　號　還是　為　參加　知道　地址

Lesson 14 ■ *Birthdays and Celebrations*

# Progress Checklist

After this lesson, you should be able to use Chinese to:

( ) ask/tell dates and days of the week,

( ) ask someone when their birthday is and how old they are,

( ) tell someone when your birthday is and how old you are,

( ) invite someone to a birthday party.

# Lesson 15  Location and Position
# 第十五課 地點和位置

## I. Listening Exercises

**15-1** Listen to Liang Zhi's introduction of his dorm. Draw a floor plan based on what you hear.

**15-2** Choose whether each statement below is true or false according to Liang Zhi's introduction.

1. His dorm is on the third floor.    True    False

2. His dorm doesn't have a kitchen.    True    False

3. His dorm is spacious.    True    False

4. The library is next to his dorm.    True    False

5. He likes to read in his dorm.    True    False

**15-3** Listen to the challenge dialogue. Though there may be some words and phrases that are unfamiliar to you, see if you can understand the general meaning by using what you have learned. Then choose whether the following statements are true or false.

1. Bao Zhizhong's dorm is small.           True     False

2. Bao Zhizhong's dorm has two bedrooms.   True     False

3. There is a kitchen in the dorm.         True     False

**15-4** Listen to the challenge dialogue again and choose the best answer for each of the following questions.

1. Where is Bao Zhizhong's dorm?
    a. By the shopping center.
    b. Behind the library.
    c. Next to Tian Jin's apartment.
    d. Next to a cafe.

2. It takes ten minutes to walk from which place to Bao Zhizhong's dorm?
    a. From the cafe.
    b. From the library.
    c. From Tiao Jin's apartment.
    d. From school.

3. Where do Bao Zhizhong and his roommate usually go to study?
    a. Bao Zhizhong studies in the library, while his roommate studies in the dorm.
    b. They both study in the library.
    c. Bao Zhizhong studies in the dorm, while his roommate studies in the library.
    d. They both study in the dorm.

Name: _____  Date: _____

## II. Character Exercises

**15-5** Write the letter of the correct position word for each question.

a. 裡邊　　b. 旁邊　　c. 對面　　d. 上邊　　e. 中間　　f. 後邊

1.  中文書在桌子的什麼地方？　____

2.  小明在他朋友的什麼地方？　____

3.  小明在文中的什麼地方？　____

4.  手機在背包的哪兒？　____

5.  中文老師在桌子的什麼地方？　____

6.  圖書館在宿舍的什麼地方？　____

**15-6** Match the Chinese characters with the corresponding Pinyin.

_____ 1. 臥室       a. chúfáng

_____ 2. 客廳       b. wòshì

_____ 3. 廚房       c. cāntīng

_____ 4. 公園       d. cānguān

_____ 5. 餐廳       e. gōngyòng

_____ 6. 洗澡       f. kètīng

_____ 7. 參觀       g. xǐzǎo

_____ 8. 公用       h. gōngyuán

## III. Grammar Exercises

**15-7** Look at the following floor plan for an apartment in the new dorm. Then answer the questions that follow.

|  廚房  |  餐廳  | 洗澡間 | 臥室 |
|---|---|---|---|
|  客廳  |  客廳  | 走廊* | 臥室 |
|       |       | 前門   |      |

Back 後 ↕ Front 前

*Note: 走廊 [zǒuláng]: hallway

1. 臥室在哪兒?

_____

2. 臥室的對面是什麼?

_____

22    Lesson 15 ■ *Location and Position*

3. 廚房和洗澡間的中間是什麼?

_____

4. 客廳和臥室的中間有什麼?

_____

5. 餐廳在客廳的哪邊?

_____

**15-8** Look at the pictures and fill in the blanks with 有, 在, 是.

1. 裙子____ 鞋子的右邊[1]。

   裙子的左邊[2] ____ 鞋子。

2. 房子的後邊____ 一棵[3]樹[4]。

   房子____ 樹的前邊。

3. 球的左邊____ 一件襯衫, 鞋子____ 球的下邊。

   襯衫____ 球的左邊, 球的下邊____ 鞋子。

*Notes:* 1. 右邊 [yòubiān]: right
2. 左邊 [zuǒbiān]: left
3. 棵 [kē]: measure word for plants
4. 樹 [shù]: tree

## IV. Comprehensive Exercises

**15-9** You work part-time at a real-estate office. Part of your job is to write introductions of houses for brochures. Write an introduction for a house in which you describe the rooms and the house's location. The following words and expressions can be used, as well other words and expressions that you have learned.

| 大門 | [dàmén] | main gate | 樓梯 | [lóutī] | stairs |
| 車庫 | [chēkù] | garage | 院子 | [yuànzi] | (court)yard |
| 地下室 | [dìxiàshì] | basement | | | |

_____

_____

_____

_____

## Progress Checklist

After this lesson, you should be able to use Chinese to:

( ) use position words to specify the relative location of something (e.g., front/back; top/under; inside/outside; left/right; beside, middle and opposite),

( ) use 在, 有, and 是 to ask/tell the location or existence of something,

( ) show people around (e.g., give a tour of your home or school).

Name: _____  Date: _____

# Lesson 16　Hobbies and Sports
# 第十六課　愛好和運動

## 🔊 I. Listening Exercises

**16-1** Listen to the dialogue. Then choose the best answer for each of the following questions.

1. Where is she going?
    a. She is going to a class.
    b. She is going to play basketball.
    c. She is going back to her dorm to make dumplings.

2. How well does he play basketball?
    a. He plays very well.
    b. He doesn't play very well.
    c. He often practices and is improving.

3. Does she like to swim?
    a. She likes to swim, and swims quite well.
    b. She likes to swim, but doesn't swim very well.
    c. She doesn't like to swim.

4. What's their plan for tonight?
    a. They will go to swim together.
    b. They will go to basketball together.
    c. They will have dumplings at her dorm.

**16-2** Listen and choose the statement that is correct.

1. a. 小美做飯做得很慢。
   b. 小美吃飯吃得很慢。

2. a. 歡歡籃球打得不太好。
   b. 歡歡籃球打得很好。

3. a. 正然作業做得很好。
   b. 正然寫字寫得很快。

Lesson 16 ■ Hobbies and Sports　25

**16-3** Listen to the challenge dialogue. Though there may be some words and phrases that are unfamiliar to you, see if you can understand the general meaning by using what you have learned. Then choose whether the following statements are true or false.

1. 張正然 and 孫信美 don't know how to play basketball.   True   False

2. 楊歡 can run very fast.   True   False

3. Today is Friday.   True   False

**16-4** Listen to the challenge dialogue again and choose the best answer for each of the following questions.

1. What are the three friends going to do at 5:00?
    a. Dine in a restaurant.
    b. Watch a movie.
    c. Play basketball in the stadium.
    d. Walk to the dorm.

2. How does 楊歡 go to meet 張正然 and 孫信美?
    a. She drives.
    b. She takes a bus.
    c. She runs.
    d. She rides a bike.

4. Why is 楊歡 almost late?
    a. She went swimming before coming.
    b. Her Literature class ended later than usual.
    c. She went to play basketball before coming.
    d. She had Chinese food before coming.

Name: _____  Date: _____

## II. Character Exercises

**16-5** Match each simplified character with its traditional form.

_____ 1. 锻     a. 籃

_____ 2. 篮     b. 體

_____ 3. 体     c. 邊

_____ 4. 图     d. 廳

_____ 5. 边     e. 圖

_____ 6. 业     f. 鍛

_____ 7. 厅     g. 業

**16-6** Write the following Pinyin sentences in Chinese characters.

1. Tā jiāode hěnhǎo.

   _____

2. Wǒ yóuyǒng yóu de hěnkuài.

   _____

3. Nǐ xiànzài yàobuyào gēn wǒmen qù duànliàn?

   _____

4. Lánqiú wǒ hái dǎde bú tài hǎo.

   _____

Lesson 16 ■ *Hobbies and Sports*   27

## III. Grammar Exercises

**16-7** Write the following sentences in Chinese, using 得 to describe actions.

1. He came very early.

2. I often eat very slowly.

3. You walk too fast.

4. He plays basketball very well.

5. My roommate goes to bed very late.

6. My mom makes dumplings very fast.

**16-8** Rewrite the following sentences so that emphasis is placed on the object of each sentence.

1. 她打籃球打得不錯。

2. 媽媽包餃子包得非常快。

3. 誰做飯做得很好?

4. 我睡覺睡得太少。

## IV. Comprehensive Exercises

**16-9** Read the following passage and then answer the questions below.

　　包健和楊中是室友。他們倆都非常喜歡運動，常常一起去健身房鍛煉。包健游泳游得很好，他是學校游泳隊[1]的，他也是楊中的游泳教練。楊中游得也不錯，可是他不常常游泳。

　　包健喜歡打籃球，他打得非常好。他也喜歡打排球[2]和乒乓球[3]。排球和乒乓球他都打得不錯。

　　他們倆也喜歡做飯。包健包餃子包得很快，也很好看。楊中做中國菜做得很好吃。他們也常常請同學們去他們的宿舍吃飯。

*Notes:*
1. 隊 [duì]: team
2. 排球 [páiqiú]: volleyball
3. 乒乓球 [pīngpāngqiú]: table tennis

1. 包健和楊中常常去哪兒?

　

2. 包健喜歡打什麼球? 他打得怎麼樣?

　

3. 楊中常游泳嗎? 他游得怎麼樣?

　

4. 他們倆做飯做得怎麼樣?

　

5. 同學們常常去他們宿舍做什麼?

**16-10** Write a short dialogue between 包健 and 楊中 based on the above reading in Activity 16-9.

_____

_____

_____

_____

_____

_____

## Progress Checklist

After this lesson, you should be able to use Chinese to:

( ) ask someone what sports they like,

( ) tell others which sports you like,

( ) ask someone how well they do a certain sport or activity,

( ) tell others how well you do certain sports or activities,

( ) talk about where, with whom, and how often you or others do a certain sport or activity.

Name: _____  Date: _____

# Lesson 17   Weather and Seasons
# 第十七課 天氣和四季

## I. Listening Exercises

**17-1**  Listen and choose the sentence that best describes the statement you hear.

1. a. Spring is coming soon, and the weather is getting warm.
   b. Winter is coming soon, and the weather is getting cold.
   c. Summer is coming soon, and the weather is getting hot.

2. a. She likes spring the most.
   b. She likes summer the most.
   c. She likes fall the most.

3. a. It is not so hot in summer here.
   b. It is very hot in summer here.
   c. It rains a lot in summer here.

4. a. It has been cold the past couple of days.
   b. It rained a lot this week.
   c. It has been extremely hot the past couple of days.

5. a. I'll go to your place during spring break.
   b. Why don't you come over during spring break?
   c. Let's go back home together during summer.

**17-2**  Listen to the dialogue between 夏華 and 春紅. Then choose whether the following statements are true or false.

1. 春紅這個學期不忙。          True     False
2. 春紅就要參加學校的籃球賽了。  True     False
3. 夏華在春假的時候要回家。      True     False
4. 夏華就要和她的好朋友見面了。  True     False

17-3 Listen to the challenge dialogue. Though there may be some words and phrases that are unfamiliar to you, see if you can understand the general meaning by using what you have learned. Then choose whether the following statements are true or false.

1. It's warm today. True False

2. Xiaoling doesn't have a winter coat. True False

3. Dazhong suggests that Xiaoling can swim during her vacation. True False

17-4 Listen to the challenge dialogue again and choose the best answer for each of the following questions.

1. Where is Dazhong going in the winter break?
    a. To Hawaii.
    b. To China.
    c. To go shopping.
    d. To New York.

2. When is Xiaoling going to travel with her parents?
    a. The weekend.
    b. Winter vacation.
    c. Summer.
    d. Spring.

3. Where is Dazhong's sister living?
    a. China.
    b. Hawaii.
    c. New York.
    d. In this city.

## II. Character Exercises

**17-5** Write the Chinese characters for the following English sentences and phrases.

1. Autumn is very warm. _____

2. Spring break _____

3. It is rainy sometimes in winter. _____

4. 100 Fahrenheit _____

5. extremely hot _____

6. Time flies. _____

**17-6** Match the Pinyin with the corresponding Chinese characters.

_____ 1. qìhòu         a. 冬天

_____ 2. dōngtiān      b. 華氏

_____ 3. fàngjià       c. 放假

_____ 4. xiàyǔ         d. 氣候

_____ 5. huáshì        e. 好久

_____ 6. nuǎnhuo       f. 下雨

_____ 7. shíjiān       g. 刮風

_____ 8. hǎojiǔ        h. 暖和

_____ 9. guāfēng       i. 見面

_____ 10. jiànmiàn     j. 時間

## III. Grammar Exercises

**17-7** Rewrite the following sentences to include a pattern from the box.

> ……的時候　　就要/快要……了　　其中

1. 我有一輛白色的車。

   _____

2. 她的弟弟今年十八歲。

   _____

3. 這個學期我有五門課。我最喜歡中文課。

   _____

4. 開車不應該打手機。

   _____

**17-8** Unscramble the following sentences by placing the characters in the correct order.

1. 下雪/這兒的/冷/,/常常/冬天/非常

   _____

2. 一百度/,/極了/會到/華氏/夏天/熱

   _____

3. 氣候/都有/這兒的/春夏秋冬/,/夏天/喜歡/我/最/其中

   _____

4. 就要/了/來/春天/,/放春假/我們/了/也/快要

   _____

Name: _____ Date: _____

## IV. Comprehensive Exercises

**17-9** Answer the following questions in Chinese.

1. 你現在怎麼樣？忙不忙？
   _____

2. 春夏秋冬，其中你最喜歡哪一個？
   _____

3. 這兒的夏天熱不熱？
   _____

4. 這兒的冬天常下雪嗎？
   _____

5. 你們就要放春假了，是嗎？
   _____

6. 春假的時候，你想做什麼？
   _____

**17-10** Write a paragraph describing the climate of the place where you come from. Try to include the following words and phrases in your paragraph. (Use at least 100 characters.)

……的時候，就要/快要……了，其中，最，極了，華氏/攝氏

_____

_____

_____

_____

Lesson 17 ■ *Weather and Seasons* 35

# Progress Checklist

After this lesson, you should be able to use Chinese to:

( ) talk about the weather and seasons,

( ) talk about the temperature,

( ) talk about which season you like/dislike the most,

( ) express that something is going to happen in the near future,

( ) write a letter.

Name: _____  Date: _____

# Lesson 18　Travel and Transportation
# 第十八課　旅行和交通

## I. Listening Exercises

**18-1**　Listen to the dialogue. Then choose the best answer for each of the following questions.

1. What will he do during spring break?
    a. He will stay here.
    b. He will go back home.
    c. He will visit a friend.
    d. He will go to the South.

2. Who will he spend the spring break with?
    a. His family.
    b. His friend who lives in New York.
    c. His friend who lives in Canada.
    d. His sister.

3. What means of transportation will he use?
    a. He will drive his brother's car.
    b. He will take an airplane and train.
    c. He will take a train and rent a car.
    d. He will take an airplane and rent a car.

4. Where will she go during spring break?
    a. She will stay here.
    b. She will go home.
    c. She will visit her sister in the South.
    d. She will visit her sister in Canada.

5. Where did he recommend that she go?
    a. To New York.
    b. To the beach.
    c. To a swimming pool.
    d. To Canada.

Lesson 18 ■ *Travel and Transportation*　37

**18-2** Listen to the questions and then give answers based on your own situation.

1. _____
2. _____
3. _____
4. _____
5. _____

**18-3** Listen to the challenge dialogue. Though there may be some words and phrases that are unfamiliar to you, see if you can understand the general meaning by using what you have learned. Then choose whether the following statements are true or false.

1. It usually takes him an hour to get to school by bike.   True   False

2. He thinks it is good exercise riding his bike to school.   True   False

3. She will go to Shanghai to visit friends during spring break.   True   False

**18-4** Listen to the challenge dialogue again and choose the best answer for each of the following questions.

1. How often does she take the bus to school?
   a. Every day.
   b. Never.
   c. Three days a week.
   d. Every Monday.

2. Why did he take the bus to school today?
   a. His car is not working.
   b. His bike is broken.
   c. His friend borrowed his bike.
   d. It is snowing today.

3. How does he go to school on snowy days?
   a. By bike.
   b. He walks.
   c. He borrows his friend's car.
   d. By bus.

Name: _____ Date: _____

## II. Character Exercises

**18-5** Write the following Pinyin sentences in Chinese characters.

1. Wǒ jiā lí xuéxiào bù yuǎn, zǒulù zhǐyào shí fēnzhōng.

   _____

2. Tā yǒushíhou zuò gōnggòng qìchē lái xuéxiào.

   _____

3. Wǒ cháng qí zìxíngchē, kěyǐ duànlian duànlian.

   _____

4. Nǐmen zěnme qù lǚxíng? Zuò huǒchē, zuò chuán, kāichē, háishì zuò fēijī?

   _____

**18-6** Match each simplified character with its traditional form.

_____ 1. 离    a. 騎

_____ 2. 车    b. 離

_____ 3. 骑    c. 聽

_____ 4. 风    d. 鐘

_____ 5. 听    e. 車

_____ 6. 边    f. 風

_____ 7. 钟    g. 邊

Lesson 18 ■ *Travel and Transportation* 39

## III. Grammar Exercises

**18-7** The following are things 文健 is going to do on different days this week. Decide what order 文健 will do each activity and write a sentence using 先, 再, and 然後 to describe the order of events.

1. 星期一：吃早飯　　上課　　游泳

   _____

2. 星期二：去圖書館　　做功課

   _____

3. 星期四：看朋友　　打電話給朋友

   _____

4. 星期五：上網　　去圖書館　　去買東西*

   _____

*Note:* 東西 [dōngxi]: things

**18-8** Complete the following sentences with a verb phrase based on the artwork clues.

1. 從美國去中國，你得_____。

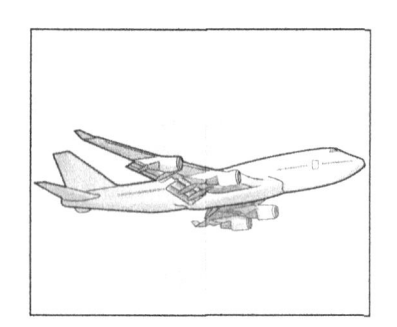

2. 春假她要_____ 回家看爸爸媽媽。

3. A: 我們怎麼去這個飯館?

   B: 我們坐＿＿＿＿＿＿＿去。

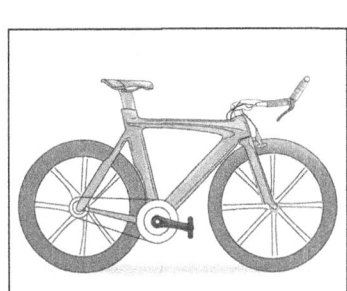

4. A: 你會＿＿＿＿＿＿＿嗎?

   B: 不會。我會＿＿＿＿＿＿＿。

## IV. Comprehensive Exercises

**18-9** Translate the following sentences into Chinese.

1. Does your younger sister live off campus? Is it far from her school?

2. I usually ride a bike to campus. When it's raining or snowing, I'll walk.

3. We want to travel to the West by train. We can look at the scenery on the way.

4. I've heard that the shore is beautiful in the South. I would like to go there to swim.

**18-10** You are chatting with your roommate about your plans for the coming summer. Write a paragraph about your plans beginning with the following sentence. Be sure to include where you are going, what you are going to do, and what transportation you will use.

我們就要放暑假了……

_____

_____

_____

_____

_____

_____

## Progress Checklist

After this lesson, you should be able to use Chinese to:

( ) ask someone if they live near or far from school, or another location,

( ) ask someone about their daily means of transportation,

( ) tell others how near or far something is,

( ) describe your daily means of transportation,

( ) describe how long it takes to go somewhere by different means of transportation,

( ) ask someone about their travel plans and describe your own travel plans,

( ) express a sequence of actions or events.

# Lesson 19  Health and Medicine
# 第十九課 健康和醫藥

## I. Listening Exercises

**19-1** Listen to the dialogue between 黃飛 and 白雪. Then choose whether the following statements are true or false.

1. 白雪來美國三個月了。　　　　　　　　　　True　　　False

2. 白雪剛*來美國的時候喜歡吃美國菜。　　　True　　　False

3. 白雪生病以後去看醫生了。　　　　　　　　True　　　False

4. 白雪現在沒有生病了。　　　　　　　　　　True　　　False

5. 白雪現在不喜歡吃美國菜了。　　　　　　　True　　　False

6. 白雪現在還不會做美國菜。　　　　　　　　True　　　False

*Note:* 剛 [gāng]: just, recently

**19-2** Listen to the dialogue. Then choose the best answer for each of the following questions.

1. Where are they going?
   a. They are going to her place.
   b. They are going to his dorm.
   c. They are going to school.
   d. They are going to the library.

2. How was she originally planning to go?
   a. She was going to ride her bicycle.
   b. She was going to take a bus.
   c. She was going to get a ride with someone.
   d. She was going to walk.

3. When did he buy his car?
   a. Today.　　b. Yesterday.　　c. Last week.　　d. Last month.

4. How long does it take to go to school by bus?
   a. An hour.　　b. Half an hour.　　c. Ten minutes.　　d. Five minutes.

**19-3** Listen to the challenge dialogue. Though there may be some words and phrases that are unfamiliar to you, see if you can understand the general meaning by using what you have learned. Then choose whether the following statements are true or false.

1. They will go to see the doctor together.        True        False

2. He has a bad stomach ache.        True        False

3. She gave him some medicine.        True        False

**19-4** Listen to the challenge dialogue again and choose the best answer for each of the following questions.

1. What is the time?
   a. 6:00 A.M.        b. 7:00 A.M.        c. 7:30 A.M.        d. 8:00 A.M.

2. What is the relationship between the two people?
   a. Roommates.
   b. Friends.
   c. Boyfriend and girlfriend.
   d. Mother and son.

3. Will he go to see the doctor today?
   a. Yes. He will go after he gets up.
   b. Yes. He will go after he finishes his test.
   c. No. He cannot go because he has a test today.
   d. No. He will just take some over-the-counter medicine.

## II. Character Exercises

**19-5** Write the Chinese characters for the following Pinyin.

1. hǎoxiàng _____
2. gǎnmào _____
3. bǐjì _____
4. fùxí _____
5. shūfu _____
6. zhǔnbèi _____
7. gǎnxiè _____
8. kǎoshì _____
9. suǒyǐ _____
10. yīshēng _____
11. chīyào _____
12. fāshāo _____

**19-6** Choose the correct simplified form for each of the following characters.

1. 頭　　a. 视　　b. 开　　c. 头
2. 發　　a. 条　　b. 双　　c. 发
3. 藥　　a. 样　　b. 药　　c. 乐
4. 筆　　a. 业　　b. 医　　c. 笔
5. 備　　a. 备　　b. 准　　c. 电
6. 醫　　a. 网　　b. 医　　c. 习
7. 餓　　a. 饿　　b. 馆　　c. 饭

## III. Grammar Exercises

**19-7** For the following sentences, first change the sentence into a question. Then give a negative answer to the question.

1. 這個夏天我就要去北京學中文了。

   Question: _____

   Negative answer: _____

2. 她做了兩個蛋糕。

   Question: _____

   Negative answer: _____

3. 我下了課以後，就去圖書館看書。

   Question: _____

   Negative answer: _____

4. 昨天我在我朋友家喝了很多酒。

   Question: _____

   Negative answer: _____

Name: _____ Date: _____

**19-8** Unscramble the following sentences by placing the characters in the correct order.

1. 我 / 還 / 吃飯 / 呢 / 沒有
   _____

2. 你 / 沒有 / 了 / 吃藥
   _____

3. 我 / 看 / 去 / 醫生 / 了
   _____

4. 你 / 在家 / 應該 / 休息 / 地 / 好好
   _____

5. 我 / 考試 / 準備 / 地 / 好好 / 得
   _____

## IV. Comprehensive Exercises

**19-9** Translate the following sentences into Chinese.

1. I bought that red skirt tonight.
   _____

2. Let's go swimming together after you recover from your illness.
   _____

3. I haven't eaten at all today, so I feel very hungry now.
   _____

4. He has read three Chinese books.
   _____

5. I traveled to the West during spring break.
   _____

**19-10** You have been staying up very late for several days and have caught a cold. You feel too sick to attend Chinese class today and plan to write a note to your teacher, which your classmate will take to class for you. Use the form below to write the note. (Use at least 80 characters.)

_____ 老師：

學生：(你的名字)

( 年　　月　　日)

## Progress Checklist

After this lesson, you should be able to use Chinese to:

(　) ask others if they are feeling well,

(　) ask others how they got sick and what symptoms they have,

(　) ask others if they have seen a doctor and if they are taking medicine,

(　) tell someone how you got sick and what symptoms you have,

(　) tell someone whether you've seen a doctor and what medicines you've taken,

(　) ask others if they have done a certain action yet and tell others if you have done something yet,

(　) indicate that a situation has changed.

# Lesson 20  Renting an Apartment
# 第二十課 看房和租房

## I. Listening Exercises

**20-1**  Listen and choose the correct English meaning for each statement you hear.

1. a. I want to move in.
   b. I want to move out.
   c. I want you to move in.
   d. I want you to move out.

2. a. I brought my girlfriend over.
   b. I went out with my girlfriend.
   c. I went to see my girlfriend.
   d. I moved in with my girlfriend.

3. a. The rent has to be paid on the first day each month.
   b. The rent has to be paid in the first month every year.
   c. The rent has to be paid at the end of each month.
   d. The rent has to be paid on the first Monday of each month.

4. a. Please come over here right now.
   b. Please leave now.
   c. Please move in now.
   d. Please come down right now.

**20-2** Listen to the dialogue between 小明 and 小謝. Then choose whether the following statements are true or false.

1. 那是小明的公寓，他們先在外面，然後進去。 True False

2. 那是小明的電視，他從家裡搬過來的。 True False

3. 小謝把房租帶來了。 True False

4. 房東太太*住在樓上。 True False

5. 小明上樓去把中文書給房東太太。 True False

*Note: 房東太太 [fángdōng tàitai]: landlady

**20-3** Listen to the challenge dialogue. Though there may be some words and phrases that are unfamiliar to you, see if you can understand the general meaning by using what you have learned. Then choose whether the following statements are true or false.

1. He wants to find a place close to where he works. True False

2. The place is close to a park. True False

3. The conversation is between a boss and an employee. True False

**20-4** Listen to the challenge dialogue again and choose the best answer for each of the following questions.

1. What kind of place is he looking for?
   a. A two-bedroom apartment.      c. A place close to the park.
   b. A dorm room on campus.        d. An apartment close to campus.

2. Where does he work?
   a. In a university.       c. At a real-estate company.
   b. In a park.             d. At a telephone company.

3. How much is the monthly rent?
   a. $300      b. $400      c. $500      d. $540

4. When can he move in?
   a. Next week.      b. In two days.      c. Anytime.      d. Next month.

## II. Character Exercises

**20-5** Write the following Pinyin sentences in Chinese characters.

1. Wǒ bǎ wǒ péngyou dàilái le.

   _____

2. Yǒu yíge rén bān chūqù le.

   _____

3. Nǐ yàobuyào bān jìnlái?

   _____

4. Qǐng nǐ bāng wǒ bǎ zhuōzi bān shàngqu.

   _____

5. Wǒ bǎ wǒde gǒu gěi wǒ nǚpéngyou le.

   _____

6. Wǒ mǎshàng xiàqu.

   _____

**20-6** Match each simplified character with its traditional form.

   ____ 1. 须     a. 過

   ____ 2. 过     b. 馬

   ____ 3. 楼     c. 須

   ____ 4. 来     d. 飯

   ____ 5. 马     e. 來

   ____ 6. 进     f. 樓

   ____ 7. 饭     g. 進

## III. Grammar Exercises

**20-7** 明學's Mom is coming to visit him the day after tomorrow. Use 把 and a directional complement to fill in the blanks in their phone conversation below. (Clues are given in parentheses.)

1. 明學：喂，是媽媽嗎？我是明學。你後天____ 我的車 ____ ____ ____ 的時候 (when you drive my car over)，也____ 我的電腦 ____ ____ ____ (move my computer over)，好嗎？

2. 媽媽：可以，要不要也____ 你的夏天衣服 ____ ____ ____ (bring your summer clothes over) 呢？

3. 明學：也好，一定要____ 那件黃襯衫 ____ ____ ____ (bring it over)，我很喜歡那件。

4. 媽媽：沒問題。噢！對了，爸爸給你買了一個新手機。

   明學：太好了！請____ 那個新手機也____ ____ ____ (bring it over) 給我吧！

5. 媽媽：我今天做了餃子，要不要也____ 一些____ ____ (bring some over) 呢？

6. 明學：太好了，我的室友要____ ____ ____ 了 (move out)，他很喜歡吃餃子，你多拿一些____ ____ (take some over) 請他吃。

7. 媽媽：那我就多 ____ 一些 ____ ____ (take some over)。

   明學：媽，我很累！我想再回 ____ (go back) 睡覺。

8. 媽媽：你昨天晚上是什麼時候從學校回 ____ (go back) 的?

   明學：我沒有車，我是 ____ ____ ____ 的 (walk back)，十一點半才 ____ ____ (come back)。再見！

**20-8** Answer the following questions about the dialogue above, using 把 and directional complements.

1. 明學的媽媽什麼時候過去看他?

2. 媽媽要帶什麼過去?

3. 明學要媽媽把黃襯衫怎麼樣?

4. 新手機是誰買的? 要怎麼處理*呢?

5. 明學昨天晚上是什麼時候回去的?

*Note: 處理 [chǔlǐ]: deal with

## IV. Comprehensive Exercises

**20-9** Use 把 and directional complements to write a story about 一隻小狗的生活 (a puppy's life). Try to write at least 8 sentences.

1. 
2. 
3. 
4. 
5. 
6. 
7. 
8.

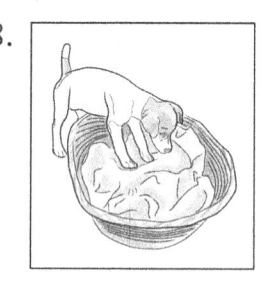

_____
_____
_____
_____
_____
_____
_____
_____

## Progress Checklist

After this lesson, you should be able to use Chinese to:

( ) describe the direction of a movement or action,

( ) ask and answer questions about an apartment (such as what rooms are in the apartment, what is allowed, and when the rent is due),

( ) ask to go and see an apartment,

( ) ask someone whether they want to come over.

# Lesson 21   Future Plans
# 第二十一課 未來計畫

## I. Listening Exercises

**21-1**  Listen to the questions. Then write your answers in Chinese characters.

1. _____

2. _____

3. _____

4. _____

**21-2**  Listen to the challenge dialogue. Though there may be some words and phrases that are unfamiliar to you, see if you can understand the general meaning by using what you have learned. Then choose whether the following statements are true or false.

1. He will travel with some friends this summer.                           True     False

2. She will do a summer internship with a company in Beijing.    True     False

3. She will visit her friends in China.                                              True     False

**21-3** Listen to the challenge dialogue again and choose the best answer for each of the following questions.

1. Where will she go this summer?
    a. Mexico.
    b. Europe.
    c. China.
    d. Home.

2. When will she leave?
    a. Tomorrow.
    b. Next month.
    c. Next Monday.
    d. In two days.

3. What will he do this summer?
    a. He will go home.
    b. He will take some classes then go to the South.
    c. He will stay here.
    d. He will go to China.

## II. Character Exercises

**21-4** Use the given character to write a word or phrase that uses the same character.

*Example:* 校   <u>學校</u>

1. 意 _____
2. 愉 _____
3. 平 _____
4. 運 _____
5. 實 _____
6. 假 _____
7. 定 _____
8. 留 _____
9. 打 _____
10. 申 _____

Name: _____ Date: _____

**21-5** Match the Chinese characters with the corresponding Pinyin.

_____ 1. 找      a. kě

_____ 2. 暑      b. zhǎo

_____ 3. 研      c. diàn

_____ 4. 可      d. bān

_____ 5. 電      e. shǔ

_____ 6. 班      f. jué

_____ 7. 業      g. yán

_____ 8. 決      h. yè

## III. Grammar Exercises

**21-6** What activities do you often do or like to do at the same time? Write six sentences using (一面……一面……/一邊……一邊……) to express things you often do at the same time or things that you like to do at the same time.

_____

_____

_____

_____

_____

_____

Lesson 21 ■ *Future Plans*   57

**21-7** Choose the correct Chinese translation for each question or statement below.

1. Are you going to China soon?
    a. 你去中國了嗎?
    b. 你去中國了沒有?
    c. 你就要去中國了嗎?

2. Have you taken the exam?
    a. 你參加考試了呢?
    b. 你參加考試了嗎?
    c. 你開始考試了嗎?

3. He is drinking coffee.
    a. 他喝了咖啡。
    b. 他喝咖啡了沒有。
    c. 他正在喝咖啡呢。

4. I haven't gone to see doctor yet.
    a. 我還沒有去看醫生呢。
    b. 我去看了醫生。
    c. 我就要去看醫生了。

Name: _____ Date: _____

## IV. Comprehensive Exercises

**21-8** What are your plans for this summer? What are your plans following graduation? Use at least 6 items from the box below and write a paragraph describing your plans for either this summer or after graduation. Try to write at least 15 sentences.

| 一面……一面……/一邊……一邊…… 了 不……了 |
| 就要……了 正在…… 然後 以前 以後 |
| 得 想 要 會 應該 覺得 把 |

Lesson 21 ■ Future Plans

## Progress Checklist

After this lesson, you should be able to use Chinese to:

( ) ask someone what they want to do after graduation or in the summer,

( ) tell someone what you want to do after graduation or in the summer,

( ) ask someone when they will graduate,

( ) tell someone when you will graduate,

( ) ask someone when they plan to leave for a trip or tell someone when you plan to leave,

( ) describe actions being performed at the same time,

( ) wish people good luck when going on a trip or starting a new job.

Name: _____ Date: _____

# Lesson 22   Arts and Culture
# 第二十二課 藝術和文化

## I. Listening Exercises

**22-1**   Listen to the passage. Then choose the best answer for each of the following questions.

1. How long has he been in Shanghai?

    a. A week.

    b. Four weeks.

    c. Two months.

    d. Four months.

2. When does class start every day?

    a. 7:30 A.M.

    b. 8:00 A.M.

    c. 8:30 A.M.

    d. 9:00 A.M.

3. What does he do every Wednesday morning?

    a. Takes Chinese class.

    b. Works in an American company.

    c. Goes to a friend's house.

    d. Visits some places in Shanghai.

4. What will he do next week?

    a. He will go sightseeing with friends.

    b. He will go out to eat with friends.

    c. He will intern at a company.

    d. He will learn how to drive in Shanghai.

**22-2** Listen to the challenge dialogue. Though there may be some words and phrases that are unfamiliar to you, see if you can understand the general meaning by using what you have learned. Then choose whether the following statements are true or false.

1. She has had lots of homework recently.          True          False

2. He tried to find good food, but didn't have much luck.          True          False

3. She is looking for a new apartment.          True          False

**22-3** Listen to the challenge dialogue again and choose the best answer for each of the following questions.

1. Where is he now?
    a. At home.
    b. In the South.
    c. In Europe.
    d. In China.

2. How long has he been there?
    a. Two days.
    b. Two weeks.
    c. A month.
    d. Two months.

3. When will he come back?
    a. Next month.
    b. Next week.
    c. In three days.
    d. Next Tuesday.

Name: _____ Date: _____

## II. Character Exercises

**22-4** Look at this lesson's Language in Use reading again. Find five words in the reading for each of the following categories and write down the characters next to each category.

1. People or things _____

2. Action _____

3. Time words _____

4. Descriptive expressions _____

**22-5** Choose the correct simplified form for each of the following characters.

1. 麗    a. 让    b. 厅    c. 丽
2. 劇    a. 剧    b. 时    c. 机
3. 東    a. 个    b. 东    c. 乐
4. 籠    a. 篮    b. 笼    c. 笔
5. 嚐    a. 尝    b. 听    c. 电
6. 興    a. 学    b. 兴    c. 识
7. 處    a. 极    b. 运    c. 处

Lesson 22 ■ Arts and Culture    63

## III. Grammar Exercises

**22-6** Rewrite the following sentences using 因為……所以…… to give a reason for the event mentioned in the sentences.

*Example:* 我的中文進步得很快。

**因為我常復習，所以我的中文進步得很快。**

1. 我沒去上課。 _____
2. 我很喜歡這裡。 _____
3. 我沒有給你打電話。 _____
4. 我今天才給你寫信。 _____
5. 我今天起床起得很早。 _____

**22-7** Answer the questions below, using 比如 to give examples.

1. Which classes do you like?

   _____

2. What places would you like to travel to?

   _____

3. What kinds of food do you like to eat?

   _____

## IV. Comprehensive Exercises

**22-8**  You are now studying Chinese in a summer program in Beijing. You have a room of your own at the dorm for foreign students. This is the third day after your arrival there. You are writing an email to your parents about your life and studies there. Because this is the first time you have traveled abroad, your parents are very concerned about you. Therefore, you should try to provide as many details as possible in your email!

爸爸、媽媽：

我到北京已經三天了。我在這兒都很好，我住在……

## Progress Checklist

After this lesson, you should be able to use Chinese to:

( ) describe your current situation and ask others about what they have been doing lately,

( ) give examples,

( ) describe causes and effects,

( ) ask someone to write to you often,

( ) send your regards and wish someone well.